D1592977

Timothy
Young Pastor

LOUISE CALDWELL • ILLUSTRATED BY **PAUL KARCH**

BROADMAN PRESS
Nashville, Tennessee

Contents

The Boy Who Loved Stories

"Tell it again, Mother, please. Tell me again about Moses."

Timothy loved the stories his mother and his grandmother told about the Jewish heroes of long ago.

"Timothy, Timothy," Mother Eunice laughed, "I have work to do. Perhaps your grandmother will have time for one more story."

Grandmother Lois smiled. "I'm glad you're learning about the great men of God, Timothy. The Jews are God's people, and we must never forget the great things God has done for us."

Grandmother sat quietly for a moment. When she spoke again her voice was troubled.

"Only a few of us in Lystra love God and try to obey him. How different Lystra would be if there were more people who loved God."

Timothy knew that what his grandmother said was true. He thought of the temple outside the city gates. Many people in Lystra visited the temple to worship before the statue of the false god they called Jupiter. The people believed in many gods, but they thought Jupiter was more powerful than any other god.

Timothy looked at his grandmother. He was glad to see her smiling again.

"Well, Timothy, we aren't the first Jews to live in a city where the people worship idols and false gods. Do you remember the story of Daniel?" Grandmother asked.

Timothy knew the story from memory. Still he loved to hear how Daniel had been faithful to God even though it meant disobeying the king. But the best part of the story was when Grandmother told how God kept Daniel safe in the lions' den.

How brave Daniel was! Timothy thought. *I wonder if I will ever be that brave for God?*

Timothy's father was not a Jew. He was a Greek, and one of the educated men of Lystra. He helped Timothy learn many things. Timothy liked to listen as his father talked with other men in Lystra. Sometimes the men told stories about traveling on the Imperial Road, a road built by the Romans. Travelers used the road when they visited the cities of Antioch and Derbe.

7

How exciting it would be to travel on roads to other cities. Maybe I can travel when I grow up, Timothy thought. Timothy also liked to imagine himself sailing on a ship to cities far away. On warm afternoons Timothy and his friends floated small stick boats on the streams near Lystra. The boys watched as the tiny boats floated down the stream and out of sight. Secretly Timothy was sure that his boat floated farther down the stream than all the other boats.

Thinkback: What have you learned about Timothy's family? What was the name of Timothy's mother? What was the name of Timothy's grandmother? What do you know about Timothy's father?

Are you like Timothy? Do you like to listen to Bible stories? Do you know some of the stories Timothy knew?

Excitement in Lystra

One day there was great excitement in Lystra. The Bible does not tell us that Timothy was present. But because Lystra was a small city, perhaps young Timothy saw and heard what happened.

Crowds of people gathered in the streets of Lystra. As the people listened, a man with a strong, clear voice said, "I have come to tell you about Jesus, the Son of God."

"Who is that stranger?" a woman asked.

"His name is Paul. The man with him is called Barnabas," someone answered.

"People of Lystra, hear me! I am here to tell you the good news of Jesus, the Son of God," Paul said.

"God? Which god?" someone asked.

"The only God, the God who loves you," Paul answered. "God, who created all things and all people, has sent us here to tell you about his Son, Jesus."

The people stood together as Paul continued to speak. Soon Paul noticed one man in the crowd who had to sit down because he was crippled. As Paul spoke,

the crippled man's face showed that he understood and believed what Paul was saying.

"Stand up!" Paul said to the crippled man. With everyone watching, the crippled man stood up. Then the man began to move. He could do more than stand. He could walk!

The people spoke in excited voices,
"That man has been crippled all his life!
It's a miracle. The strangers can perform
miracles! They cannot be men like us.
They must be gods! Yes, they are gods!"

A woman pointed to Barnabas. "That one is Jupiter," she said.

"The man who spoke must be Mercury, the god who speaks for Jupiter," others said. Even the priest at the temple of Jupiter believed that Paul and Barnabas were gods.

"No, you are wrong," Paul told the people. "We are not gods. There is only one God. We have come to tell you about Jesus, the Son of God. It is Jesus you must trust, not us."

On the streets and in the houses the people of Lystra talked about what Paul had said. In families like Timothy's there was great joy. These were the people who loved and worshiped God. For years they had waited for the Messiah. Now Paul and Barnabas were preaching that he had come. Timothy's mother and his grandmother believed that Jesus was God's Son.

But the joy in Timothy's family soon turned to sorrow. Jews from the cities of Antioch and Iconium came to Lystra, not to speak for Jesus, but to turn the people of Lystra against Paul and Barnabas.

Just as quickly as the people had
believed Paul and Barnabas to be gods,
they turned against the two missionaries.
Angry, shouting men and women threw
rocks at Paul and Barnabas and drove
them from the city. Paul was hit by so
many stones that the mob left, thinking he
was dead.

But Paul was not dead. Soon he and Barnabas were on their way again, telling the good news of Jesus in other cities.

Even though the missionaries had been driven from Lystra, they knew that some in the town believed in Jesus. Paul and Barnabas prayed for the believers, "Help the new Christians in Lystra, Lord. Give them wisdom. Make them brave for Jesus."

Paul's and Barnabas' prayer was answered. The new Christians in Lystra met in homes to pray and to praise God. They prayed that Paul and Barnabas could tell more people about Jesus. They also prayed for the missionaries to be able to return to Lystra. Before long Paul and Barnabas visited in Lystra again for a short time.

Thinkback: Who preached about Jesus in Lystra?

Why did Paul and Barnabas have to leave Lystra?

What did the new Christians do after the missionaries left?

Paul Returns to Lystra

It was a happy day for the Christians in Lystra. Paul, their brave missionary friend, had returned after a long time of traveling. Eagerly the people crowded around him. "Tell us about your travels. Have you told many people about Jesus?" they asked.

"There are many new Christians in the cities of Derbe and Antioch and Iconium. The churches there are growing stronger, just like your church here in Lystra," Paul answered.

As his friends listened, Paul told about sailing to Antioch and traveling to the city of Jerusalem. Everywhere he went Paul always told the good news of Jesus. "But there are still so many people to tell, so many cities to visit," Paul said.

"Where is Barnabas?" the people asked.

"He left with young John Mark for the island of Cyprus while Silas and I began our journey here," Paul answered.

Paul was glad to be back with his friends in Lystra. For many hours he talked with the new Christians, teaching them and answering their questions.

Young Timothy became a special friend to Paul. He liked to hear about Paul's travels. He especially liked to hear about how Jesus spoke to Paul on the Damascus Road. "How strong Timothy's faith is for one so young," Paul told Silas.

"Your faith in Jesus is strong like your mother's faith," Paul told his young friend. "Be thankful for a wise mother and grandmother who taught you to love and obey God."

The Christians in Lystra knew that it would soon be time for Paul and Silas to leave them. "How can we help with your work?" the church members asked the missionaries.

"We have been praying for a new helper," Paul answered. "What about young Timothy? Would he be a good helper?"

"Yes, Timothy is ready to work hard for Jesus. Many people here in Lystra have learned about Jesus from Timothy. Even the Christians in Iconium speak well of him. Timothy is young, but he has known the ways of God since he was a child," the church members said.

Paul and Silas were sure that Timothy would be a good missionary helper. The church members who knew Timothy best were sure that Timothy was ready. What would Timothy's answer be?

"I must pray before I answer," Timothy told Paul. "If I travel with you, it must not be only because I want to go or because you have asked me to go. But if I go I must go because God wants me to go."

Alone by the stream where he had played as a boy, Timothy prayed. He also

prayed with his mother and with his grandmother. At last Timothy knew what God wanted him to do. "Yes, I will go with you," he told Paul and Silas.

But as he prepared to leave on his first missionary trip, Timothy was surprised by how he felt. "How can I be happy and sad at the same time?" Timothy asked his mother.

Eunice also loved and served God, and she answered Timothy wisely, "I understand how you feel, my son. I am happy and sad, too. I am happy that God has chosen you to help tell people about Jesus. But I love you, and it makes me sad to know that you will be away from me. Every day you are away I will pray for you."

The day came when the missionaries were ready to leave. Paul spoke kindly to Timothy's mother, "I will help and teach Timothy all I can. I have no children of my own, but I will treat Timothy as I would my own son."

Timothy's new work for Jesus was beginning.

Thinkback: Why were the Christians at Lystra so happy to see Paul?

What missionary came with Paul to Lystra? Where was Barnabas?

What made Timothy decide to travel with Paul and Silas?

How did Timothy feel about his decision?

New Cities, New Friends

Paul, Silas, and Timothy left Lystra and began to travel north. The trip was sometimes hard, but it was always exciting for Timothy.

Paul carried a letter from the Christians in Jerusalem. In each church the missionaries visited, Paul read and explained the letter. Timothy listened closely as Paul answered questions and taught the people. As Timothy listened to Paul, he learned how to tell people about Jesus.

Timothy made many new friends as the missionaries traveled. Some of the people he met reminded Timothy of the friends he missed in Lystra. It always made Timothy glad to remember that his Christian friends in Lystra were praying for his new friends and for him. It was a nice feeling to know that his old and new friends had something in common—they loved Jesus.

Timothy was happy when a new friend joined the missionary team. Luke was a doctor. Timothy remembered that Paul had nearly been killed by an angry mob on his first visit to Lystra. *It will be good to have a doctor traveling with us,* Timothy thought.

Glad as they were to have a doctor, Paul and Silas and Timothy welcomed Luke for another more important reason.

Luke's Christian faith and great kindness
made the others love him. Sometimes
Timothy thought, as he watched Doctor
Luke, *Jesus must have been like that.*

After a long journey the travelers
arrived in Troas, a city near the seacoast.
While they were in Troas God spoke to
Paul in a dream, or vision. Paul knew that
he and his helpers were being sent by God
to Macedonia.

Macedonia was across the Aegean Sea, and ships sailed there often. The two-day trip across the sea was exciting for Timothy. Looking out over the blue sea, the young man wondered what the cities of Macedonia would be like. Timothy prayed for God's help in the new work. He was glad to know that at home his mother was praying for him, too.

The first Macedonian city visited by the missionaries was Philippi. They found Lydia and some other women worshiping God by the river in Philippi. Lydia and others in her household became the first people in Philippi to trust in Jesus and be baptized.

"I have room at my house. Please stay with me while you are here," Lydia said to the missionaries. Gladly the men agreed. It was a happy time for Timothy.

But soon there was trouble in Philippi. Paul and Silas were even put in jail for preaching. The missionaries moved on to other cities, but the trouble continued. Jews who did not believe in Jesus followed Paul to each new city. Finally in Beroea Paul said to Silas and Timothy, "If I leave you, the trouble may stop. I will go on to Athens. Stay awhile with the Christians here. They need your help."

By now Timothy had become more than Paul's young helper. He did the work of a missionary pastor, traveling to places where Paul knew a pastor's help was needed. Sometimes Timothy took letters from Paul to the Christians in different places.

Timothy missed Paul and was glad when they could be together. But Timothy knew there were many cities to visit, churches to help, and people who needed to hear about Jesus. Timothy was still a young man, but he had learned well. He was ready to work for Jesus wherever he was needed.

Thinkback: Do you think Timothy liked traveling with Paul?

Can you name another missionary friend of Timothy?

How did Paul and Timothy meet Lydia?

What do you think Timothy did when he was afraid? when he was sad? when he was happy?

Hard Work for a Young Pastor

Ephesus was a great city. Crops grew well on the rich farm land nearby. Ephesus was also near the sea. Ships sailed to and from the city every day. Some ships brought goods from Macedonia and Greece to be sold in Ephesus. Many businessmen lived in the busy city.

Near Ephesus was a large and beautiful temple built by those who worshiped a

goddess they called Diana. The building was made of white marble and decorated with gold.

Because idol worship was so popular in Ephesus, Paul stayed longer in that city than in any other city he visited. Paul preached in the smaller towns near Ephesus as well as in the city itself. Soon there were many new Christians in Ephesus.

But there was trouble in Ephesus. Some people began to worry because there were

so many new followers of Jesus in the city. Paul and Timothy worried about the new followers, too. Paul and Timothy knew they needed a pastor to help them be strong and faithful for Jesus in times of trouble.

They prayed and the Christians in the church at Ephesus prayed. Soon they knew that Timothy was the man God had chosen to lead the church. In a special worship service Timothy was ordained for his new work.

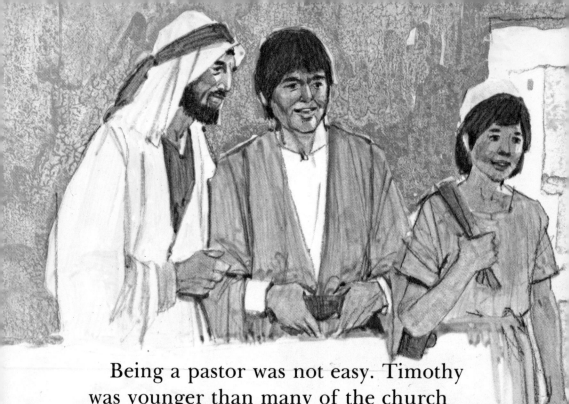

Being a pastor was not easy. Timothy was younger than many of the church members, but it was up to him to set a good example. Timothy knew that he had to do more than just tell people how Christians should live. His actions had to show how a Christian should live.

Teaching was an important part of a pastor's work. Timothy must have taught the Christians what Paul said about prayer: "Pray not just for yourselves or for those who are like you, but for all people. Remember that God loves all people and wants everyone to know about Jesus."

Timothy knew that other people in Ephesus were watching to see how the Christians acted. He told the church members something else Paul had written him: "You must not argue and quarrel with each other. When you come to worship you must not dress or behave like those who worship at the temple of Diana."

Choosing good leaders and teachers in the church was important. Pastor Timothy helped the people choose good and faithful men as deacons. He warned them against listening to those who taught false ideas.

Even for Christians money was sometimes a problem. Timothy taught church members to share with widows and others who needed money. Those who were rich were reminded by the young pastor to be generous with their money.

"Do not expect money to make you happy. God has given us the things we need to be happy. Doing good to others is more important than being rich with money," Timothy taught. Paul had taught Timothy this.

Timothy knew that he would never be rich. Sometimes at night the young pastor may have thought about the home where he had lived as a boy in Lystra. *What would my life have been like if I had never left Lystra?* Timothy wondered.

But Timothy was not sorry. His life for Jesus was happy and busy, and there was still so much work to do.

Thinkback: What did Timothy have that was more important than money?

What do you have that is more important than money?

Missionary Letters

Trips were hard in the days of Timothy. Travel was slow and often dangerous. Still the missionaries traveled from city to city telling the good news of Jesus to all who would listen.

41

But even missionaries who worked as
hard as Paul and his helpers could not tell
all the people about Jesus. God had
another, better plan. God planned for
churches.

Wherever the missionaries went they
helped the new Christians start churches.
The church in Lystra and the one in
Ephesus were two of these churches.
When the missionaries moved on to other
cities, the church members kept on telling
people about Jesus.

Paul knew that the churches he started
needed help. As often as he could, he
visited the churches. But Paul also helped
the churches in other ways.

Sometimes Paul sent Timothy or another missionary pastor to visit and help a church. Other times Paul wrote letters. The letters were a way of teaching the church members what Paul could not go and teach them himself. God's Holy Spirit was always guiding Paul as he wrote the letters.

Timothy often delivered letters for Paul. Sometimes Timothy was with Paul when letters were written. Perhaps Timothy helped by copying some of the letters.

Timothy was with Paul when the letter to the church at Philippi was written. Timothy must have remembered how he enjoyed staying at the home of Lydia in Philippi.

Thessalonica was a city Paul and his helpers visited after they left Philippi. Timothy was sent back to Thessalonica to teach and bring news of the church back to Paul. Later Timothy was with Paul when he wrote letters to the Thessalonians.

Even though most of Paul's letters were written to churches, two of his letters were written to Timothy. Timothy received the letters in Ephesus.

Paul's second letter to Timothy was written from Rome. Paul had been put in prison there for preaching about Jesus. This letter to Timothy was probably the last letter Paul ever wrote.

Paul addressed the letter to "Timothy, my beloved child." The letter showed his great love for Timothy. Soon, Paul knew, Timothy might have to suffer for Jesus. Paul wanted Timothy to be brave and faithful no matter what happened.

The Bible does not tell us how Timothy felt when he read Paul's last letter. Perhaps Timothy felt the same way he felt when he left Lystra to travel with Paul. Then Timothy had felt happy and sad at the same time.

Knowing that his friend Paul might soon be killed must have filled Timothy with sadness. But remembering the good years he had shared with his missionary friend must have filled Timothy with great joy. Paul was not afraid to die. He encouraged Timothy to continue preaching.

After his last letter from Paul, Timothy probably went on teaching people about Jesus. He had promised God to teach about him and he kept his promise.

Thinkback: Why did Paul write letters to churches?

How many letters did Paul write to Timothy?

Reflections

Timothy is often remembered because two books in the Bible are called by his name. Those are the letters written by Paul to Timothy. Can you find the two letters in your Bible?

Now that you know Timothy better, what do you remember about him?

Timothy, the boy

Who taught Timothy about God?

What did Timothy do that you like to do, too?

Timothy, the missionary helper

Do you think Timothy tried to be like Paul?

Do you ever try to be like someone else?

Do you try hard to be like Jesus?

Timothy, the pastor

How was Timothy a good pastor?

What have you learned from your pastor?

The name Timothy means "one who honors God." How did Timothy honor God? How do you honor God?

SOME NEW TESTAMENT PLACES

48